Mary's Little Instruction Book

Mary's Little Instruction Book

LEARNING FROM THE WISDOM OF THE BLESSED MOTHER

BY EILEEN ELIAS FREEMAN

WARNER BOOKS

A Time Warner Company

Warner Books, Inc., 1271 Avenue of the Americas, New York, NY 10020

 A Time Warner Company

Printed in the United States of America
First Printing: May 1995
10 9 8 7 6 5 4 3 2 1

Library of Congress Cataloging-in-Publication Data
Freeman, Eileen E.
        Mary's little instruction book : learning from the wisdom
        of the Blessed Mother/by Eileen Elias Freeman.
            p.   cm.
        ISBN 0-446-67181-9
        1. Mary, Blessed Virgin, Saint—Quotations 2. Bible—Quotations.
I. Title.
    BT605.5.F74 1995   95-1885
    232.91—dc20   CIP

All quotations from the scriptures have been taken from the New Revised Standard Version, copyright © 1989 by the Division of Christian Education of the National Council of the Churches of Christ in the United States of America and used by permission.

Book design by Eileen Elias Freeman

Cover design by Julia Kushnirsky

✠

*I dedicate this book with love and gratitude to the entire
faith community of St. Anne's Episcopal Church,
Tifton, Georgia, and to the
Reverend H. Jacoba Hurst, Rector,
a priest forever according to the order of Melchizedek,
who have ministered to me the healing grace of Christ
and taught me more than I have ever been able
to share with them.*

Contents

Introduction

*T*his book is a compendium of the wisdom of Mary, the Mother of Jesus. It contains words she has said in the scriptures, as well as messages she has given in our own day, according to the beliefs of many. Some of these sayings are historical, some are apocryphal.

Some are still a mystery.

For me, the most important words the Virgin Mary has ever said are "Do whatever *He* tells you." It happened at the wedding reception in Cana, the party that John tells us Jesus also attended with his disciples. When the wine ran out too early, the butler looked to Mary for help. Why? Perhaps she had agreed to put on the wedding reception for the happy couple. Or maybe she was a close relative or friend of the family. The disconsolate servant probably tapped her on the shoulder and pointed out that the wine was gone—and what was he going to do now? *Oy!*

This was a sad event! Wedding parties in Jesus's day could go on for days. To run out of wine prematurely was a serious breach of hospitality. But Mary was not at all ruffled by the dire tidings. She turned to her son Jesus and told him, simply and with total trust, "They have no more wine." Jesus's answer seemed to indicate that providing wine for partygoers was not what either he—or his mother—had been put on earth to do.

And yet—without even batting an eye, confident that she knew her son's mind, Mary pointed out Jesus to the wine waiter and said, "Do *whatever* He tells you." And Jesus provided 180 gallons of the best bubbly for all, in response to his mother's request for help.

If ever a lesson was needed today, surely it is *"Do what He tells you."* We have for much too long done what *we* wanted to do, and we suffer as a result, because our choices are often poor. That is why, for me, the wisdom of the Blessed Mother and her most important role is to point to her Son, to say, "Do whatever He tells you," and then to step back, out of the field of vision, so we can do it. But in the end, Jesus, who loves and honors his mother, calls her forth publicly as an example to all people of true wisdom of heart, of holiness, of strength of spirit; and he responds to her confident prayer.

For nearly two millennia, people have looked to Mary as a model of all that a loving human life can be when illuminated by the grace of God. Some centuries have seen her for the strong, loving and wise woman she is. Others have trivialized her and protected her with lace and candles. And a few, alas, have made her into virtually a goddess, which, I am certain, has never pleased either God or her.

Mary's glory is that she is human—and only human. But from the first days of Christianity she has been seen as a special woman, because she was the mother of Jesus; and because Christians worship Jesus as God, Mary became the Mother of God. She was seen as the eternal virgin, the temple of the Holy Spirit, the woman clothed with the sun in the Book of Revelation, the woman who never turned her face from the light of God, who heard the angel's message and did what God asked of her, who loves and cares for the world as only a mother can.

I have always felt it is in the scriptures and in the wisdom of the early Christian writers that we best understand the mission of Jesus's mother. She was a woman of her time and culture. But her heart-filled love and compassion make her, in a very real way, the mother of us all.

Mary's Little Instruction Book includes not only the wisdom of the early Christian communities, but certain words attributed to her by recent visionaries from around the world—the United States, Syria, Bosnia, Italy, Argentina, and elsewhere. It is difficult to know just how many of these words might really be communications from Mary, and many people are divided about whether humans can, through the providence of God, communicate God's messages to the world today.

I believe, as the author of the letter to the Hebrews has said, that "we are surrounded by . . . a great cloud of witnesses." In other words, those who lived on earth are still witnesses to what we say and do. They are aware of all that goes on throughout the Earth, and they see our lives through the divine prism, with great clarity and an enhanced perspective that is beyond us. Elsewhere the scripture itself testifies that Elijah and Moses appeared to Jesus and spoke with him about his passion (Luke 9:30ff.). And no one doubts that Moses and Elijah had died centuries before Jesus lived on earth. I believe, therefore, that genuine apparitions of Mary are possible.

The difficult part in all of this is discernment. In *Touched by Angels* and *Angelic Healing,* I have discussed issues pertaining to spiritual discernment, because we must not, cannot, accept uncritically any spiritual teaching that presents itself, no matter how attractive, without testing it. I believe that God has spoken with authority in the sacred scriptures, and at our peril we accept visions and teachings that contradict the word of God. And that word tells us that "every good tree bears good fruit, but the bad tree bears bad fruit." (Matthew 7:17) So I believe that if the words that people attribute to Mary are indeed from God, then the fruits of people taking those words to their hearts will be sweet and nourishing, even if the fruits take years or centuries to ripen.

In the end, even testing cannot guarantee that a visionary like Bernadette of Lourdes really saw Mary and spoke with her. After all, out of our own hearts, by grace, we can produce words that are loving and wise. It must always remain a matter of faith, because, as Paul points out, "We walk by faith, not by sight." And yet no one who has been to places like Lourdes, who has seen the pilgrims cured and people's hard hearts melted and turned to God, can doubt that something of God is happening there.

About this book:

Like its predecessor, *The Angels' Little Instruction Book,* this volume uses verses from the Bible to place the sayings from/about its subject in context. Sometimes the Hebrew or Christian scriptures can add more depth to what little we know of Mary, who liked to "ponder things in her heart" and who thought more than she spoke. To these I have added a line or two showing the relationship of the two scriptures, or the saying and the scripture.

In this way, even if one can never prove that Mary has said the things attributed to her, or if what has been said about her is historically true, at least it can be shown that they are in accord with the scriptures by which she lived her life. And at the end I have added some notes about the sources for these contemporary apparitions attributed to the Blessed Mother, so the reader can place the sayings in their historical and cultural perspective.

What is important is not that we put Mary on an exalted pedestal of our own making. God did that when she was invited to become the mother of Jesus. What is important is that in Mary we see the heights to which humanity—charged, filled, and overflowing with the fire and grace of God—can rise.

May our response to grace always be like hers—loving, strong, and wise—and always saying *Yes!* to God.

Eileen Elias Freeman
The AngelWatch™ Foundation, Inc.
November 1994

The Life of Mary According to Sacred Scripture and Ancient Writings

The books of the Bible are not the only ancient testimony to the life of the Virgin Mary. The *Nativity of Mary,* sometimes called the *Protoevangelium of James,* is an ancient Christian writing that tells of Mary's own birth and childhood. Although the *Nativity* was never accepted as Holy Writ, it was still widely believed to be a sort of biography of the Blessed Mother, and has influenced many Christian traditions, such as the names of Mary's parents (Anna and Joachim), the tradition that Mary was a virgin of the Temple, and the lovely "Cherry Tree Carol," widely sung at Christmas. The ancient prayers and litanies also add to our understanding.

And behold an angel of the Lord came to Anna and said, "Anna, the Lord has heard your prayer. You shall conceive and bear a child, and your offspring shall be spoken of in all the world."

—Nativity of Mary 4.1

And this is the boldness we have in him, that if we ask anything according to his will, he hears us. And if we know that he hears us in whatever we ask, we know that we have obtained the requests made of him.

—1 John 5:14-5

The Nativity of Mary is an apocryphal gospel of great antiquity that preserves many legends and stories of Mary's infancy and childhood. According to tradition, Anna and Joachim were a childless couple of a Jewish priestly family. Anna asked God for a child, and, as 1 John reminds us, God answered her prayer.

And Anna said, "As the Lord my God lives, if I bear a child, whether male or female, I will bring it as a gift to the Lord my God, and it shall serve him all of its days."

—Nativity of Mary 4.1

❀

Hannah made this vow: "O Lord of hosts, if only you will look on the misery of your servant, and remember me, and not forget your servant, but will give to your servant a male child, then I will set him before you as a nazirite until the day of his death.

—1 Samuel 1:11

It was not uncommon for parents to dedicate their children to God. According to the author of the work, Anna herself offered her child to the Lord, as did Hannah, the mother of Samuel the prophet. But the difference is, I think, that Anna simply wanted a baby, any baby, while Hannah asked for a son.

In her ninth month Anna gave birth to a daughter, as the angel had said. And she nursed the child and called her Mary.

—Nativity of Mary 5.2

In due time Hannah conceived and bore a son. She named him Samuel, for she said, "I have asked him of the Lord."

—1 Samuel 1:20

The name Mary, in Hebrew Maryam or Miriam, has never been adequately translated. It may come from a word meaning "bitter" or it may derive from a term implying richness. I think the latter is probably more likely. Having given birth to a healthy child, Anna's life had, for her, become richer than ever—and so had the life of the world.

Day by day Mary grew strong;
when she was six months old,
her mother stood her on the ground
to see if she could stand. And Mary walked
seven steps and returned to her mother.

—Nativity of Mary 6.1

❧

The child grew and became strong, filled with wisdom;
and the favor of God was upon him.

—Luke 2:40

The writer of the Nativity of Mary knew well the Gospel of Luke, and took pains to
show that in many ways Mary was like her son Jesus—spiritually mature at an early
age. The seven steps that Mary took are symbolic of the attainment of Lady Wisdom or
Sophia, whose house contains seven pillars (Proverbs 9:1).

On Mary's first birthday, Joachim brought Mary to the priests and they blessed her, saying, "O God of our ancestors, bless this child and give her a name renowned forever among all generations."

—Nativity of Mary 6.2

❀

I will make of you a great nation, and I will bless you, and make your name great, so that you will be a blessing.

—Genesis 12:2

Mary has been seen as the mother of Christianity, because she was the mother of Jesus. Through him, she has indeed become the mother of a great nation, and her name has been a blessing to millions of people through the centuries.

And they brought her to the chief priests, and they blessed her, saying, "O God of the heavenly heights, look down on this child and bless her with a supreme and unsurpassable blessing."

—Nativity of Mary 6.2

❀

The Lord bless you and keep you; the Lord make his face to shine upon you, and be gracious to you; the Lord lift up his countenance upon you, and give you peace.

—Numbers 6:24-6

I wonder what sort of blessing the priests of the temple had in mind when they blessed the child Mary. What did they consider "supreme and unsurpassable"? Was it just hyperbole, or did they know that Mary was destined to bear the King of Ages in her womb?

When Mary was three, her parents brought her to the temple. And the priest took her and placed her on the third step of the altar, and the Lord God put grace upon her and she danced for joy with her feet, and the whole house of Israel loved her.

—Nativity of Mary 7.3

❀

Then shall the young women rejoice in the dance, and the young men and the old shall be merry. I will turn their mourning into joy, I will comfort them, and give them gladness for sorrow.

—Jeremiah 31:13

This wonderful passage captures the very heart of Mary, who not only understood her destiny, but danced with happiness.

And her parents went home marveling and praising God, because Mary did not turn back after them.

—Nativity of Mary 8.1

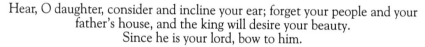

Hear, O daughter, consider and incline your ear; forget your people and your father's house, and the king will desire your beauty.
Since he is your lord, bow to him.

—Psalms 45:10-11

The psalm given above is said to be a wedding psalm. Tradition says that Mary, from her earliest youth, saw herself as the handmaid of God, and desired no other as her "husband."

And Mary lived in the temple
nurtured like a dove, and received food
from the hand of an angel.

—Nativity of Mary 8.1

❁

Then Elijah lay down under the broom tree and fell asleep. Suddenly an angel touched him and said to him, "Get up and eat." He looked, and there at his head was a cake baked on hot stones, and a jar of water. He ate and drank, and lay down again.

—*1 Kings 19:5-6*

The nativity story reminds us of Mary's purity; the images of dove and angelic food demonstrate that her life was holy. Elijah was fed by an angel in a time of distress. But for Mary, angel food was her way of life. According to the tradition, she lived in the Temple until she grew to adulthood, when she was placed under the protection of Joseph, an older man and a widower with grown children of his own.

*In the sixth month the angel
Gabriel was sent by God to a town
in Galilee called Nazareth, to a virgin engaged
to ... Joseph, of the house of David. The
virgin's name was Mary.*

—Luke 1:26-7

The angel replied, "I am Gabriel. I stand in the presence of God, and I have
been sent to speak to you and to bring you this good news."

—Luke 1:19

*Gabriel's words to Zechariah introduce this heavenly messenger, one of the seven great
angels of Jewish antiquity. Only the greatest of the angels was good enough to announce
the news to Mary.*

*And he came to her and said,
"Greetings, favored one!
The Lord is with you."*

—Luke 1:28

But the angel said to the women, "Do not be afraid; I know that you are
looking for Jesus who was crucified. He is not here; for he has been raised, as
he said. Come, see the place where he lay."

—Matthew 28:5-6

*In the Bible, an angel always begins a message with "Do not be afraid." But to Mary,
Gabriel gave greetings, and I think it was because Mary's heart was too full of love to
contain any fear.*

*But she was much perplexed
by his words and pondered
what sort of greeting this might be.*

—Luke 1:29

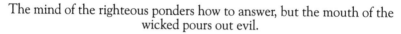

The mind of the righteous ponders how to answer, but the mouth of the
wicked pours out evil.

—Proverbs 15:28

*When Gabriel came to Zechariah to tell him he was going to be a father, the priest was
terrified and scorned the message as impossible. Mary, by contrast, was reflective, and
thought before she spoke.*

The angel said to her,
"Do not be afraid, Mary, for
you have found favor with God."

—Luke 1:30

"Blessed be the Lord God of Israel, for he has looked favorably
on his people and redeemed them."

—Luke 1:68

The favor of God—imagine what it must have been like to be told by an angel that you
had found favor with God, that God had taken note of you and was especially pleased.
The parallel song of Zechariah reminds us that Mary was not just favored personally,
but was part of a special people.

> *"And now, you will conceive
> in your womb and bear a son, and you
> will name him Jesus."*
>
> —Luke 1:31

❊

And the angel of the Lord said to the woman, "You shall conceive and bear a son. No razor is to come on his head, for the boy shall be a nazirite to God from birth. It is he who shall begin to deliver Israel from the hand of the Philistines."

—Judges 13:3, 5

The birth of special people is often presaged by angels. Both Mary and the mother of Sampson saw angels who came to teach them about their children. Just as Samson was sent to deliver Israel from Philistine oppression, so Jesus was sent to deliver Israel from spiritual oppression.

"He will be great, and will be called the Son of the Most High, and the Lord God will give to him the throne of his ancestor David."

—Luke 1:32

For a child has been born for us, a son given to us; authority rests upon his shoulders; and he is named Wonderful Counselor, Mighty God, Everlasting Father, Prince of Peace.

—Isaiah 9:6

Gabriel's words to Mary must have recalled to her this prophecy from Isaiah about the coming of the Messiah. Surely Gabriel's words would also have brought even more questions to Mary's mind.

"He will reign over the house of Jacob forever, and of his kingdom there will be no end."

—Luke 1:33

❀

His authority shall grow continually, and there shall be endless peace for the throne of David and his kingdom. He will establish and uphold it with justice and with righteousness from this time onward and forevermore. The zeal of the Lord of hosts will do this.

—Isaiah 9:7

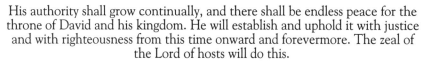

Mary's wonder and amazement increased as Gabriel continued the message. Surely there could be no doubt as to what the angel meant by "Son of God." Her son would be the eternal king over the hearts and minds of his people.

*Mary said to the angel,
"How is this to take place, since I am a
virgin?"*

—Luke 1:34

❁

Thus says the Lord, the Holy One of Israel, and its Maker:
Will you question me about my children, or command me concerning the
work of my hands?

—Isaiah 45:11

*Mary's answer to Gabriel is a marvel of intelligent inquiry. When the angel of God told
Sarah she would have a child, she laughed at the message. When the angel told
Zechariah his wife would bear a son, he scorned the angel. Mary simply asked an
intelligent question: How?*

The angel said to her, "The Holy Spirit will come upon you, and the power of the Most High will overshadow you; therefore the child to be born will be holy; he will be called Son of God."

—Luke 1:35

And those in the boat worshiped him, saying,
"Truly you are the Son of God."

—Matthew 14:33

The angel's words to Mary were prophetic; Jesus's disciples hailed him as Son of God during his earthly life. Yet to his mother, he was also the Son of Mary.

"And now, your relative Elizabeth in her old age has also conceived a son; and this is the sixth month for her who was said to be barren."

—Luke 1:36

Then one [of the angels] said, "I will surely return to you in due season, and your wife Sarah shall have a son." Now Abraham and Sarah were old, advanced in age. So Sarah laughed to herself. The Lord said to Abraham, "Why did Sarah laugh?" At the set time I will return to you, in due season, and Sarah shall have a son."

—Genesis 18:10ff.

The angel's message to Mary must have reminded her of another angel's message long before, to a distant ancestor, for Mary came from an ancient priestly family.

"For nothing will be impossible with God."

—Luke 1:37

Is anything too wonderful for the Lord?

—Genesis 18:14

I often wonder if Gabriel added this last line to the message just because his news that Mary would give birth to the Messiah was so difficult to believe. After all, Mary was just a simple young woman from a Jewish priestly family. Nothing but a sign from the past of her own people could have made it seem real. After the angel had left, Mary even journeyed to see Elizabeth just to prove to herself that the message of Gabriel was real.

Then Mary said, "Here am I, the servant of the Lord; let it be with me according to your word." Then the angel departed from her.

—Luke 1:38

❀

Now the Lord came and stood there, calling as before, "Samuel! Samuel!" And Samuel said, "Speak, for your servant is listening."

—1 Samuel 3:10

Gabriel's word strongly indicated the nature of God's plan, but they did not compel Mary to give in. Had she said no to the message of Gabriel, human history would have been written differently. But instead she answered freely, Yes! and accepted the invitation that changed the world forever.

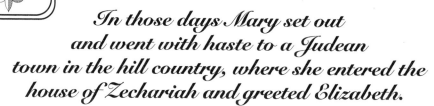

*In those days Mary set out
and went with haste to a Judean
town in the hill country, where she entered the
house of Zechariah and greeted Elizabeth.*

—Luke 1:39-40

❀

"Come, you that are blessed by my Father, inherit the kingdom prepared for
you from the foundation of the world; for I was hungry and you gave me food,
I was thirsty and you gave me something to drink, I was a stranger and you
welcomed me, I was naked and you gave me clothing, I was sick and you took
care of me, I was in prison and you visited me."

—Matthew 25:34-6

*Mary's visit no doubt involved two reasons: first, to see for herself that the words of
Gabriel about her cousin were indeed true; second, to rejoice with her and help her
during her months of pregnancy.*

When Elizabeth heard Mary's greeting, the child leaped in her womb. And Elizabeth was filled with the Holy Spirit and exclaimed, "Blessed are you among women, and blessed is the fruit of your womb."

—Luke 1:41-2

❋

While he was saying this, a woman in the crowd raised her voice and said to him, "Blessed is the womb that bore you and the breasts that nursed you!" But he said, "Blessed rather are those who hear the word of God and obey it!"

—Luke 11:27-8

Elizabeth's greeting reminds us that somehow God had already prepared her for Mary's visit. Somehow she knew that Mary was destined by God to have a special role in the history of the human race.

"And why has this happened to me, that the mother of my Lord comes to me? For as soon as I heard the sound of your greeting, the child in my womb leaped for joy."

—Luke 1:43-4

❦

Listen to me, O coastlands, pay attention, you peoples far away! The Lord called me before I was born, while I was in my mother's womb he named me.

—Isaiah 49:1

Tradition says that when Mary greeted Elizabeth, the older woman's child, who would be known as John the Baptist, was commissioned to be a prophet of God while still in his mother's womb. The prophecy from Isaiah reminds us that other prophets have felt the same call. Elizabeth's own prophecy, to call Mary "the mother of my Lord," was no less important.

*"And blessed is she who believed
that there would be a fulfillment of what was
spoken to her by the Lord."*

—Luke 1:45

We walk by faith, not by sight.

—2 Corinthians 5:7

Elizabeth praises Mary for her faith. And, indeed, Mary's faith must have been extraordinary. To believe that God would effect a pregnancy in her without human participation, and to believe that her son would be the Son of God, too, and the king of ages—who could not forgive her had she doubted? But she never did.

And Mary said, "My soul magnifies the Lord, and my spirit rejoices in God my Savior, for he has looked with favor on the lowliness of his servant."

—Luke 1:46-8a

Hannah prayed, "My heart exults in the Lord; my strength is exalted in my God. My mouth derides my enemies, because I rejoice in my victory."

—1 Samuel 2:1

The Hebrew scriptures are full of stories of women who asked God to send them a child, in spite of obstacles such as age. Hannah, the mother of the prophet Samuel, sang a hymn of joy at the fulfillment of her petition that recalls the opening words of Mary's Magnificat.

"Surely, from now on all generations will call me blessed. "

—Luke 1:48b

Many women have done excellently, but you surpass them all.

—Proverbs 31:29

Mary's Magnificat continues with her acknowledgment that God's favor has in some way set her apart. Yet the word here translated as "blessed" means also "happy," so Mary is confirming her faith that this miracle in her life will be a sign of rejoicing.

> *"For the Mighty One has done
> great things for me, and holy is his name.
> His mercy is for those who fear him from
> generation to generation."*
>
> —Luke 1:49-50

I will cause your name to be celebrated in all generations; therefore the
peoples will praise you forever and ever.

—Psalms 45:17

*Mary's soliloquy reminds us that the reason she is so happy is because of the wonderful
things God has done for her. She goes on to remind us that God's mercy is not something
meant just for her, but is for all people in all ages to come.*

*"He has shown strength
with his arm; he has scattered the proud
in the thoughts of their hearts."*

—Luke 1:51

Talk no more so very proudly, let not arrogance come from your mouth; for the Lord is a God of knowledge, and by him actions are weighed. The bows of the mighty are broken, but the feeble gird on strength.

—1 Samuel 2:3-4

Hannah's song of joy continues to echo the Magnificat, as both women praise the Almighty who delivers the poor in spirit.

"He has brought down the powerful from their thrones, and lifted up the lowly; he has filled the hungry with good things, and sent the rich away empty."

—Luke 1:52-3

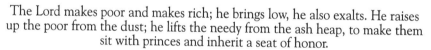

The Lord makes poor and makes rich; he brings low, he also exalts. He raises up the poor from the dust; he lifts the needy from the ash heap, to make them sit with princes and inherit a seat of honor.

—1 Samuel 2:7-8a

Hannah's song and Mary's Magnificat continue to flow together, uniting two women of very different centuries. Mary's song is our own, too, whenever we stop to count our blessings.

"He has helped his servant Israel, in remembrance of his mercy, according to the promise he made to our ancestors, to Abraham and to his descendants forever."

—Luke 1:54-5

❦

Then God said to Abraham, "I have made you the ancestor of a multitude of nations. I will establish my covenant between me and you, and your offspring after you throughout their generations, for an everlasting covenant, to be God to you and to your offspring after you."

—Genesis 17:7

Mary also remembered her ancestor in faith Abraham as she sang her song of joy. Abraham is seen throughout the Bible as the model of someone who heard the voice of God, demanding of him great faith, and who put his trust totally in God's providence.

*And Mary remained with her
about three months and then returned
to her home.*

—Luke 1:56

So they remained for a long time, speaking boldly for the Lord, who testified
to the word of his grace by granting signs and wonders to be done
through them.

—Acts 14:3

*What did Mary do for those three months with Elizabeth? Did she sew baby things and
get a layette ready? Probably. But I also like to think that she talked long and hard with
Elizabeth, the two of them sharing about the children growing in their wombs, marveling
at the wonders of God. Perhaps they did not "speak boldly," but their quiet conversations
were surely filled with grace and wisdom.*

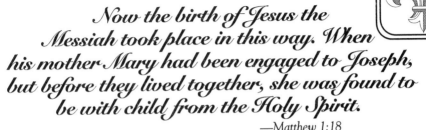

Now the birth of Jesus the Messiah took place in this way. When his mother Mary had been engaged to Joseph, but before they lived together, she was found to be with child from the Holy Spirit.

—Matthew 1:18

❀

Therefore the Lord himself will give you a sign. Look, the young woman is with child and shall bear a son, and shall name him Immanuel.

—Isaiah 7:14

When I was a teenager, the unmarried young woman who got "in the family way" was considered a disgrace forever. The parents of my generation were not forgiving. Mary, too, may have had to endure much pain when her pregnancy began to manifest itself. Yet there is no word in the scriptures of her anger or any bitterness at being misunderstood. Instead we marvel at the silent calm and total trust that all would work out as the angel Gabriel had said to her.

Her husband Joseph, being a righteous man and unwilling to expose her to public disgrace, planned to dismiss her quietly.

—Matthew 1:18

Plead with your mother, plead—for she is not my wife, and I am not her husband—that she put away her whoring from her face, and her adultery from between her breasts, or I will strip her naked and expose her as in the day she was born, and make her like a wilderness, and turn her into a parched land, and kill her with thirst.

—Hosea 2:2-3

The law of Israel was harsh when it came to adultery—a woman could be stoned to death by her husband and the community. Mary faced this real possibility, for an engagement was as binding as a marriage in her era. Thank God Joseph was a just man!

But just when he had resolved to do this, an angel of the Lord appeared to him in a dream and said, "Joseph, son of David, do not be afraid to take Mary as your wife, for the child conceived in her is from the Holy Spirit."

—Matthew 1:20-1

❀

In a dream, in a vision of the night, when deep sleep falls on mortals, while they slumber on their beds, then God opens their ears.

—Job 33:16

The scriptures never speak of Mary's dreams, only of her thoughts and musings. But guidance was given to Joseph concerning her, through the message of an angel, so that the plan of God could go forward.

All this took place to fulfill what had been spoken by the Lord through the prophet: "Look, the virgin shall conceive and bear a son, and they shall name him Immanuel," which means, "God is with us."

—Matthew 1:22-3

Therefore the Lord himself will give you a sign. Look, the young woman is with child and shall bear a son, and shall name him Immanuel. He shall eat curds and honey by the time he knows how to refuse the evil and choose the good.

—Isaiah 7:14-5

The words of Isaiah have long been the quintessential prophecy of the birth of Jesus. Although Isaiah's prophecy does not specifically say that the mother is a virgin, the word has been understood in this way since the earliest days of the Christian church.

When Joseph awoke from sleep, he did as the angel of the Lord had commanded him; he took her as his wife, but had no marital relations with her until she had borne a son; and he named him Jesus.

—Matthew 1:24-5

❋

Your wife will be like a fruitful vine within your house; your children will be like olive shoots around your table. Thus shall the man be blessed who fears the Lord.

—Psalms 128:3

Who was Joseph, Mary's husband? We know so little of him, except that he was a carpenter and a just man. Tradition says he was an elderly widower with grown children who took Mary to protect her virginity. Matthew seems to say that after the birth of Jesus, Mary and Joseph had a normal marital relationship; the text, however, is open to other interpretations.

In those days a decree went out from Emperor Augustus that all the world should be registered. Joseph also went . . . to Bethlehem . . . with Mary, to whom he was engaged and who was expecting a child.

—Luke 2:1, 4-5

❦

Take a census of the whole congregation of Israelites, in their clans, by ancestral houses, according to the number of names, every male individually.

—Numbers 1:2

What a long and arduous trip it must have been for Mary, whose pregnancy was well advanced—at least five days on the road from dawn to dusk. Yet there was no escaping the demands of the law. Trusting in God, she went with Joseph. Tradition says she rode a donkey, but nothing in scripture suggests this. She may well have walked the entire way.

While they were there, the time came for her to deliver her child. And she gave birth to her firstborn son and wrapped him in bands of cloth, and laid him in a manger, because there was no place for them in the inn.

—Luke 2:6-7

Before she was in labor she gave birth; before her pain came upon her she delivered a son. Who has heard of such a thing? Who has seen such things? Shall a land be born in one day? Shall a nation be delivered in one moment? Yet as soon as Zion was in labor she delivered her children.

—Isaiah 66:7-8

What did Mary think when Joseph came to her with the news that there was no room in the inn? Surely by then she had already gone into labor. The only available shelter—a stable—would have been cold and dirty. But in such a place, Mary gave birth to Jesus.

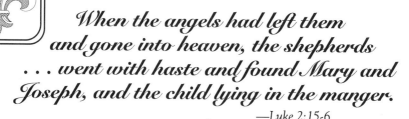

When the angels had left them and gone into heaven, the shepherds . . . went with haste and found Mary and Joseph, and the child lying in the manger.

—Luke 2:15-6

Tell me, you whom my soul loves, where you pasture your flock, where you make it lie down at noon; for why should I be like one who is veiled beside the flocks of your companions? If you do not know, O fairest among women, follow the tracks of the flock, and pasture your kids beside the shepherds' tents.

—Song of Songs 1:7-8

The angels announced the birth of Jesus to the shepherds who guarded their flocks on the slopes around Bethlehem. What did Mary think as she lay there on the straw, wrapped in a blanket, nursing her newborn, when suddenly the shepherds, curious, fearful, excited, trooped in to see her and her baby?

When the shepherds saw the child,
they made known what had been
told them about him, and all who heard it
were amazed. But Mary treasured all their
words and pondered them in her heart.

—Luke 2:19

❁

My soul is satisfied as with a rich feast, and my mouth praises you with joyful
lips when I think of you on my bed, and meditate on you in the watches
of the night; for you have been my help, and in the shadow of your
wings I sing for joy.

—Psalms 63:5-7

When the shepherds came to the stable, they shared with Mary and Joseph all that the
angels had told them. Mary saw their words as an enormous gift, something to be
treasured; and she reflected on what they might mean for herself and her son, Jesus.

*After eight days had passed,
it was time to circumcise the child;
and he was called Jesus, the name given by
the angel before he was conceived
in the womb.*

—Luke 2:21

❀

You shall circumcise the flesh of your foreskins, and it shall be a sign of the covenant between me and you. Throughout your generations every male among you shall be circumcised when he is eight days old.

—Genesis 17:11-2

The covenant of circumcision goes back to the time of Abraham. Circumcision was the rite that officially made a male an Israelite.

When the time came for their purification, they brought him up to Jerusalem to present him to the Lord, and they offered a sacrifice according to . . . the law of the Lord.

—Luke 2:22, 24

When the days of her purification are completed, whether for a son or for a daughter, she shall bring to the priest at the entrance of the tent of meeting a lamb for a burnt offering, and a pigeon or a turtledove for a sin offering.

—Leviticus 12:6

Mary and Joseph came to the temple after Jesus's birth to fulfill the requirements of their faith. The scriptures go on to say that if the mother could not afford to offer a lamb, she could offer two pigeons instead. Could Mary afford the lamb? And did Mary realize that her son, Jesus, would be called the "Lamb of God who takes away the sin of the world" (John 1:29)?

*Guided by the Spirit, Simeon
came into the temple; and when the
parents brought in the child Jesus, Simeon took
him in his arms and praised God, saying,
"Master, now you are dismissing your
servant in peace . . . for my eyes have
seen your salvation."*

—Luke 2:25a, 27-30

❈

One thing I asked of the Lord, that will I seek after: to live in the house of the
Lord all the days of my life, to behold the beauty of the Lord,
and to inquire in his temple.

—Psalms 27:4

*An old tradition says that Mary was brought up in the Temple. If so, then perhaps
Simeon was an old friend who had known her as a child.*

And the child's father and mother were amazed at what was being said about him.

—Luke 2:33

Then they brought to him a demoniac who was blind and mute; and he cured him, so that the one who had been mute could speak and see. All the crowds were amazed and said, "Can this be the Son of David?"

—Matthew 12:22-3

Mary's son was a source of amazement from his earliest youth. As a child, he would confound the learned teachers in the Temple, and as a man, he would be a source of wonder and surprise at his teachings and miracles. And here we see that even Mary, the quiet woman who pondered things in her heart, was amazed at what was prophesied about him.

Then Simeon blessed them and said to his mother Mary, "This child is destined . . . to be a sign that will be opposed so that the inner thoughts of many will be revealed—and a sword will pierce your own soul too."

—Luke 2:34-5

Is it nothing to you, all you who pass by? Look and see if there is any sorrow like my sorrow.

—Lamentations 1:12

Simeon's prophecy of tragedy to Mary is reflected in the Lamentations passage, which has long been applied metaphorically to her, who, like Mother Jerusalem, saw her son put to death.

***When they had finished
everything required by the law
of the Lord, they returned to Galilee, to their
own town of Nazareth.***

—Luke 2:39

I delight to do your will, O my God; your law is within my heart. I have told
the glad news of deliverance in the great congregation; see, I have not
restrained my lips, as you know, O Lord.

—Psalms 40:8-9

*Joseph and Mary were descended from the priestly tribes of Israel and were devout Jews.
They observed the commandments faithfully, from their hearts, not mechanically or by
rote. In their time, they would not have been required to go to Jerusalem itself to present
their son to the Lord, yet they made the long journey because of their faith.*

On entering the house, [the Magi] saw the child with Mary his mother; and they knelt down and paid him homage. Then, opening their treasure chests, they offered him gifts of gold, frankincense, and myrrh.

—Matthew 2:11

May the kings of Tarshish and of the isles render him tribute, may the kings of Sheba and Seba bring gifts. May all kings fall down before him, all nations give him service.

—Psalms 72:10-1

The visit of the Magi must have occasioned even more wonder for Mary—imagine, to have rich and exotic people from a distant land come to pay homage to your child!

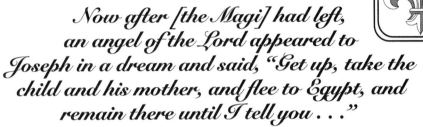

Now after [the Magi] had left, an angel of the Lord appeared to Joseph in a dream and said, "Get up, take the child and his mother, and flee to Egypt, and remain there until I tell you . . ."

—Matthew 2:13-4

Thus says the Lord: A voice is heard in Ramah, lamentation and bitter weeping. Rachel is weeping for her children; she refuses to be comforted for her children, because they are no more.

—Jeremiah 31:15

What a dangerous journey to undertake, and yet how necessary! For Herod, in his old age, had become a sadistic monster, murdering anyone he felt had designs on his throne, including the infants of Bethlehem. What did Mary's family think when they disappeared? Surely she must have told them where they were going so they wouldn't worry.

When Herod died, an angel of the Lord suddenly appeared in a dream to Joseph in Egypt and said, "Get up, take the child and his mother, and go to the land of Israel, for those who were seeking the child's life are dead." Then Joseph got up, took the child and his mother, and went to Israel.

—Matthew 2:19-21

❋

When Israel was a child, I loved him, and out of Egypt I called my son.

—Hosea 11:1

The flight into Egypt is Joseph's time to shine; and yet it was because of Mary and the need to protect her child—which was not his at all—that he took such risks. Was Gabriel the angel behind all these events, or was it Joseph's own guardian angel?

Now every year Jesus's parents went to Jerusalem for the festival of the Passover. And when he was twelve years old, they went up as usual for the festival.

—Luke 2:41-2

Now before the festival of the Passover, Jesus knew that his hour had come to depart from this world and go to the Father. Having loved his own who were in the world, he loved them to the end.

—John 13:1

Jesus's parents, as religious Jews, undertook the journey to Jerusalem every year for Passover. Mary brought him up well, to know his faith and the religious traditions of his people. In the early Church, as today, he is seen as the ultimate paschal lamb, slaughtered for the sake of the people.

When the festival was ended and they started to return, the boy Jesus stayed behind in Jerusalem, but his parents did not know it. When they did not find him . . . they returned to Jerusalem to search for him.

—Luke 2:43, 45

❄

What do you think? If a shepherd has a hundred sheep, and one of them has gone astray, does he not leave the ninety-nine on the mountains and go in search of the one that went astray? And if he finds it, truly I tell you, he rejoices over it more than over the ninety-nine that never went astray.

—Matthew 18:12-3

Did Mary blame herself when she realized Jesus was missing? After all, she had been made the custodian and mother of the Son of God. Was Joseph angry or fearful? Parents today would understand such emotions. I think this was one of Mary's great tests of faith.

After three days they found him in the temple, sitting among the teachers, listening to them and asking them questions. When his parents saw him they were astonished; and his mother said to him, "Child, why have you treated us like this? Look, your father and I have been searching for you in great anxiety."

—Luke 2:46, 48

❦

A child who loves wisdom makes a parent glad.
—Proverbs 29:3

Once again, Mary asks a question—not "How?" this time, but "Why?" Yet in her anxious questioning, Mary is still the loving mother, concerned to know what prompted her son to cause his parents worry.

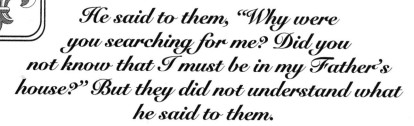

He said to them, "Why were you searching for me? Did you not know that I must be in my Father's house?" But they did not understand what he said to them.

—Luke 2:49-50

❀

Jesus said, "Do not let your hearts be troubled. Believe in God, believe also in me. In my Father's house there are many dwelling places. If it were not so, would I have told you that I go to prepare a place for you?"

—John 14:1-2

Perhaps Mary was too much the human mother this time. Jesus, with a maturity that leaves us astounded in our own day, reminded his mother that he had a vision even she could not share. And for once, all Mary's ponderings were not enough. She could not grasp the immensity of what her twelve-year-old son had just told her.

*Then he went down with them
and came to Nazareth, and was
obedient to them. His mother treasured all
these things in her heart.*

—Luke 2:51

Children, obey your parents in the Lord, for this is right.

—Ephesians 6:1

*After Mary and Joseph found him in the Temple, Jesus obeyed his parents and came
home with them. And the text reminds us that obedience to his parents was a notable
virtue. It's awesome to consider that the God of the universe was obedient to Mary and
to Joseph. He probably fetched water, sharpened Joseph's tools, fed the goats, and cleaned
the privy. Were these the memories Mary treasured, of the Son of God helping her set the
table for the Sabbath dinner?*

Then Jesus's mother and brothers came to him . . . And he was told, "Your mother and your brothers are standing outside, wanting to see you." But he said to them, "My mother and my brothers are those who hear the word of God and do it."

—Luke 8:18-21

Your word is a lamp to my feet and a light to my path.
—Psalms 119:105

Mary quickly became an archetype for all followers of Jesus. Here, Jesus holds her motherly role up to all and invites the crowd to have such a love and devotion as she had. Mary followed her son during the course of his ministry, mostly staying in the background.

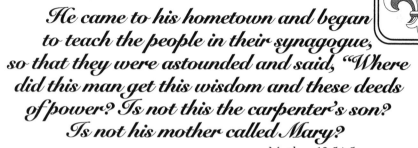

*He came to his hometown and began
to teach the people in their synagogue,
so that they were astounded and said, "Where
did this man get this wisdom and these deeds
of power? Is not this the carpenter's son?
Is not his mother called Mary?*

—Matthew 13:54-5a

❀

Nathanael said to him, "Can anything good come out of Nazareth?"
Philip said to him, "Come and see."

—John 1:46

*I wonder if Mary minded having her son referred to as the son of Mary. The neighbors
seem to use Mary's name almost as a source of reproach, as if to say, "He's got Mary for
a mother—how could he be anyone special?" But Mary knew better.*

*On the third day there was
a wedding in Cana of Galilee, and the mother
of Jesus was there. Jesus and his disciples
had also been invited to the wedding.*

—John 2:1-2

Jesus said to them, "The wedding guests cannot fast while the bridegroom is with them, can they? As long as they have the bridegroom with them, they cannot fast."

—Mark 2:19

Weddings were important social and religious events in Jesus's day. He probably danced and ate and drank with the men while Mary and the women led the bride in dancing, too. I like to think, in view of what happened, that Mary was probably the one who had organized the reception for the happy couple's families.

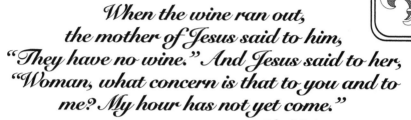

When the wine ran out,
the mother of Jesus said to him,
"They have no wine." And Jesus said to her,
"Woman, what concern is that to you and to
me? My hour has not yet come."

—John 2:3-4

❀

And do not keep striving for what you are to eat and what you are to drink, and do not keep worrying. For the nations of the world strive after all these things, and your Father knows that you need them. Instead, strive for his kingdom, and these things will be given to you as well.

—Luke 12:29-31

It has always been important to me that when the wine ran out, it was to Jesus that Mary turned. She could have just as easily have complained to the steward, "Why didn't you order more, you stupid idiot! I told you it wouldn't be enough." Instead, she asked her son to do something he was unaccustomed to doing—provide a miracle for a purely secular reason, so the family would not be embarrassed.

His mother said to the servants, "Do whatever he tells you."

—*John 2:5*

❀

"Why do you call me 'Lord, Lord,' and do not do what I tell you?
—*Luke 6:46*

Mary's role in the life of Jesus's followers has always been like this: to point to her son, to tell us to do whatever he tells us—and then to step back so he can act. What wonderful trust she had in her son, to know instinctively that he would do something appropriate to save the situation. She probably experienced a great sense of relief when she knew that Jesus had actually arrived at the wedding celebration.

*Jesus did this, . . .and revealed
his glory; and his disciples believed in
him. After this he went down to Capernaum
with his mother, brothers, and disciples; and
they remained there a few days.*

—John 2:11-2

❊

But Ruth said, "Do not press me to leave you or to turn back from following
you! Where you go, I will go; where you lodge, I will lodge; your people shall
be my people, and your God my God."

—Ruth 1:16

*After Mary stepped back, Jesus had six thirty-gallon crocks filled with water, and then
turned them into the best quality wine. And after the party was over, he and his mother
and the rest of the company set off together. Mary apparently accompanied Jesus on a
number of his preaching journeys. It must have been a hard life at first, without any
assurance that a roof would be over their heads at night. But for a woman who had
given birth in a stable, perhaps it wasn't so much of a hardship after all.*

*Meanwhile, standing near the cross
of Jesus were his mother, and his
mother's sister, Mary the wife of Cleopas,
and Mary Magdalene.*

—John 19:25

O that my head were a spring of water, and my eyes a fountain of tears, so that
I might weep day and night for the slain of my poor people!

—Jeremiah 9:1

*It's interesting to note the company that Mary kept in her grief and distress.
Her sister was with her, surely a loving gesture, but so was Mary Magdalene, the
ex-hooker whose life Jesus had transformed by his love. The Blessed Mother's love
was as all embracing as her son's love was.*

When Jesus saw his mother
and the disciple whom he loved standing beside
her, he said to his mother, "Woman, here is
your son."

—John 19:26

As a mother comforts her child, so I will comfort you;
you shall be comforted in Jerusalem.

—Isaiah 66:13

Jesus, with a loving gesture, thought to provide for his mother, even as he was dying.
What a compassionate thing to do! In Jesus's day, the woman who was widowed and
without children was often in a desperate economic situation.

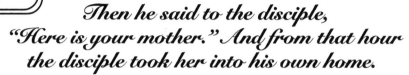

*Then he said to the disciple,
"Here is your mother." And from that hour
the disciple took her into his own home.*

—John 19:27

❊

Kindness to a parent will never be forgotten, and will be credited to you
against your sins; in the day of your distress it will be remembered
in your favor.

—Ecclesiasticus 3:14-5

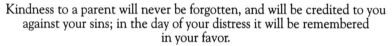

*Jesus's words to John have been interpreted metaphorically or spiritually as being a gift of
his mother to all humanity. Jesus says to everyone of Mary: "Here is your mother."*

*When they had entered the city,
[the apostles] went to the room upstairs
where they were staying. All of them were
constantly devoting themselves to prayer,
together with certain women, including Mary
the mother of Jesus, as well as his brothers.*
—Acts of the Apostles 1:13-4

❋

Devote yourselves to prayer, keeping alert in it with thanksgiving.
—Colossians 4:2

*Mary rarely speaks, but no matter what the occasion she is always there, quietly sharing,
joining in. Here, in the Upper Room, she keeps vigil with the disciples of Jesus, waiting
for the special gift of the Spirit that her son had promised.*

When the day of Pentecost had come . . . divided tongues, as of fire, appeared among them, and a tongue rested on each of them. All of them were filled with the Holy Spirit and began to speak in other languages, as the Spirit gave them ability.

—Acts of the Apostles 2:1, 3-4

❊

Is not my word like fire, says the Lord, and like a hammer
that breaks a rock in pieces?

—Jeremiah 23:29

The fire of the divine Spirit is a transforming flame that takes the human spirit and burns
all the dross away, leaving pure gold behind. Mary's spirit, already pure gold, proclaimed
God's wonders in languages she never learned to people she never knew.

A great portent appeared in heaven: a woman clothed with the sun, with the moon under her feet, and on her head a crown of twelve stars. She was pregnant and was crying out in birth pangs, in the agony of giving birth.

—Revelation 12:2

❀

Therefore the Lord himself will give you a sign. Look, the young woman is with child and shall bear a son, and shall name him Immanuel.

—Isaiah 7:14

This passage, in which the woman represents the early Christian Church, is often applied to the Virgin Mary, who appears as a type of the Church. It reminds us that Mary is indeed a mother, a woman who understands the pain of all mothers.

*Then another portent appeared
in heaven: a great red dragon, with
seven heads and ten horns, and seven diadems
on his heads. Then the dragon stood before the
woman who was about to bear a child, so he
might devour her child as soon as it was born.*

—Revelation 12:3-4

❀

Discipline yourselves, keep alert. Like a roaring lion your adversary the devil
prowls around, looking for someone to devour.

—1 Peter 5:8

*The scriptures are silent about Mary's personal struggle against evil, yet we know she
must have had to deal with anger and rage over the crucifixion of her son Jesus. Yet she
fought the impulse to hate, to despair. She forgave, she overcame evil with love.*

And she gave birth to a son, a male child, who is to rule all the nations with a rod of iron. But her child was snatched away and taken to God and to his throne; and the woman fled into the wilderness, where she has a place prepared by God.

— Revelation 12:5-6

❧

Fear and trembling come upon me, and horror overwhelms me. And I say, "O that I had wings like a dove! I would fly away and be at rest; truly, I would flee far away; I would lodge in the wilderness."

—Psalms 55:5-7

Revelation again reminds us that Mary serves as the image of Mother Church. But I like to think of this text in connection with the flight into Egypt, that terrible journey undertaken in haste to save the life of the infant Jesus from the wrath of Herod.

Then the dragon was angry with the woman, and went off to make war on the rest of her children, those who keep the commandments of God and hold the testimony of Jesus.

—Revelation 12:17

❀

For these things I weep; my eyes flow with tears; for a comforter is far from me, one to revive my courage; my children are desolate, for the enemy has prevailed.

—Lamentations 1:16

We associate Mary with peace and tranquillity, but she is also a woman of deep passion who cares intensely about all people. Like a loving mother, she longs for them to know and love her son, and she weeps because of the coldness of the world. In her apparitions she often speaks of her pain because people turn away from God's love.

Holy Virgin of virgins . . .
Mother of good counsel . . .
Virgin most wise . . .
Mother most pure . . .
Virgin most faithful . . . pray for us.

—Litany of Loreto

❀

Then the kingdom of heaven will be like this. Ten bridesmaids took their lamps and went to meet the bridegroom. Five of them were foolish, and five were wise. When the foolish took their lamps, they took no oil with them; but the wise took flasks of oil with their lamps.

—Matthew 25:1-4

The Litany of Loreto is a prayer in the Roman Catholic tradition that addresses the Blessed Virgin under many scriptural and traditional titles and asks her to pray for us.

Mirror of justice . . .
Seat of wisdom . . .
Vessel of honor . . .
Cause of our joy . . .
Mystical rose . . . pray for us
—Litany of Loreto

❀

I am a rose of Sharon, a lily of the valleys.
—*Song of Songs 2:1*

The words of the Song of Songs are a love poem, celebrating the marriage of King Solomon. But for two millennia the figure of the bride has been applied to Mary in a mystical way, celebrating her response to the call of God, not for physical union but for spiritual betrothal.

Tower of David . . .
Tower of ivory . . .
Ark of the covenant . . .
Gate of heaven . . .
Morning star . . . pray for us.

—Litany of Loreto

Your neck is like an ivory tower, your eyes are pools in Heshbon, by the gate of Bath-rabbim. Your nose is like a tower of Lebanon, overlooking Damascus. Your head crowns you like Carmel, and your flowing locks are like purple; a king is held captive in the tresses. How fair and pleasant you are, O loved one, delectable maiden!

—Song of Songs 7:4-6

The images from the Song of Songs continue, as the litany praises the woman who kept herself for God alone.

Queen of angels . . .
Queen of prophets . . .
Queen of martyrs . . .
Queen of virgins . . .
Queen of peace . . . pray for us.

—Litany of Loreto

❀

From ivory palaces stringed instruments make you glad;
daughters of kings are among your ladies of honor;
at your right hand stands the queen in gold of Ophir.

—Psalms 45:8-9

Mary is hailed as queen of heaven, not because she stands beside her son as an equal,
but because he has chosen to lift her up as a model for all of how human life is filled
and transfigured by God's grace.

The Wisdom of Mary from Modern Apparitions

PRAYER

Pray! Pray! Pray!

—*Scottsdale, 1988*

❖

"Stay awake and pray that you may not come into the time of trial; the spirit
indeed is willing, but the flesh is weak."

—*Matthew 26:41*

*The encouragement to pray is perhaps the most frequent statement that Mary has made
in the various apparitions of the twentieth century. Sometimes the words are specific, but
most often they are just the heartfelt sentiments of a woman who knows that all things
are possible through prayer.*

*I would like to ask for the future,
for families with children to work
and pray together with their children daily
to become stronger in the spirit.*

—Medjugorje, 1989

We must no longer be children, tossed to and fro and blown about by every wind of doctrine, by people's trickery, by their craftiness in deceitful scheming. But speaking the truth in love, we must grow up in every way into him who is the head, into Christ . . .

—Ephesians 4:14-15a

Prayer in the family is something that Mary urges at every possible opportunity. Here she not only asks for families to pray together but for parents to help their children to grow strong in living a life rooted in the spiritual rather than the material.

*Love, pray with your heart,
be humble, and keep Jesus at the very
center of your life.*

—*Scottsdale, 1988*

❀

Rejoice always, pray without ceasing, give thanks in all circumstances; for this is the will of God in Christ Jesus for you.

—*1 Thessalonians 5:16-18*

As a mother raising a most unusual child, Mary was probably aware of Jesus every minute of the day. Whether he was at the synagogue learning his aleph-beth or helping Joseph sand planks in the carpenter shop, Jesus was the center of Mary's world.

Pray, pray, with all your strength.
—*Fatima, 1917*

❀

You shall love the Lord your God with all your heart,
and with all your soul, and with all your strength.
—*Deuteronomy 6:5*

Mary's message in Fatima invites listeners to turn their hearts to God with more energy and effort than ever before. The world is in desperate need of prayer and sacrifice, and only when our hearts are grounded in prayer can we be ready to meet its needs.

*Love is the simplest, most beautiful,
and purest form of prayer.*

—Scottsdale, 1988

No one has ever seen God; if we love one another,
God lives in us, and his love is perfected in us.

—1 John 4:12

*Mary is often spoken of as the model of perfect contemplative prayer—the heart that,
instead of praying to God with many devout words, simply looks in God's direction with
a loving glance and lives in the divine presence. Prayer must be filled with love if it is to
change our hearts and transform the world.*

I see your weariness, little ones.
Please, I invite you not to give up,
but to continue in your prayer. Prayer is so
vital . . . for your world.

—*Medjugorje, 1986*

❀

By day the Lord commands his steadfast love, and at night his song
is with me, a prayer to the God of my life.

—*Psalms 42:8*

Mary sees the world in a way we cannot—through the eyes of her son Jesus. She has
seen the wars and conflicts, the movements and the catastrophes on earth since she was
taken out of this world. She knows better than any of us the value and the need for
prayer, not only for ourselves but for the entire planet.

I have come to earth in order to teach you to pray with love.

—Medjugorje, 1986

❀

He said to them, "When you pray, say: Father, hallowed be your name.
Your kingdom come. Give us each day our daily bread.
And forgive us our sins, for we ourselves forgive everyone indebted to us.
And do not bring us to the time of trial."

—Luke 11:2-4

The disciples asked Jesus to teach them how to pray. The prayer of Mary is, I think, a different prayer; it is the prayer of a mother who loves her children and wants all of them to grow up and be happy.

*I do not need two hundred
Our Fathers. It is better to pray one, but
with the desire to encounter God.*

—Medjugorje, 1985

"When you are praying, do not heap up empty phrases as the Gentiles do; for they think that they will be heard because of their many words. Do not be like them, for your Father knows what you need before you ask him."

—Matthew 6:7-8

Mary echoes the words of her son Jesus, who reminds us that quality, not quantity, is what counts before God.

In prayer, you will find the solution for every situation, even if it is unsolvable.

—Medjugorje, 1984

No testing has overtaken you that is not common to everyone. God is faithful, and he will not let you be tested beyond your strength, but with the testing he will also provide the way out so that you may be able to endure it.

—1 Corinthians 10:13

Gabriel said to Mary that with God nothing is impossible. I think that must have been one of the many things Mary pondered over the years. The angel's message taught her that no situation is without a solution, no matter how serious, because with God all things are indeed possible.

When you pray, you are
very beautiful, like flowers
after a snow, vivid with beauty in their
indescribable colors.

—Medjugorje, 1986

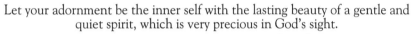

Let your adornment be the inner self with the lasting beauty of a gentle and
quiet spirit, which is very precious in God's sight.

—1 Peter 3:4

Mary sees the human spirit from a very different vantage point than we do ourselves.
We are too close to our own souls to see how we look as we move to greater
transformation in our lives. Mary, who sees with the clear eyesight of heaven,
perceives the beauty of the soul who prays with love.

I invite you to read the Bible every day within the family. Display it so it will incite you to read it and to pray.

—Medjugorje, 1984

But as for you, continue in what you have learned and firmly believed, knowing from whom you learned it, and how from childhood you have known the sacred writings that are able to instruct you for salvation through faith in Christ Jesus.

—2 Timothy 3:14-15

Mary has always been a great proponent of family values and instilling in children a desire to know more about the loving God who has created us. In Medjugorje, many families have small shrines or prayer areas where the Bible is displayed on a special stand and families gather around it daily to read it and pray.

God has a plan for each one of you.
Without prayer, you will not be able to
understand it.

—Medjugorje, 1987

❀

Although I am the very least of all the saints, this grace was given to me to bring to the Gentiles the news of the boundless riches of Christ, and to make everyone see what is the plan of the mystery hidden for ages in God who created all things.

—Ephesians 3:8-9

From her vantage point, Mary surely understand how God's plan for her life transformed the face of the world and its history. But she reminds us that each of us is part of the divine plan, and no one else can make the contribution that God expects from each of us.

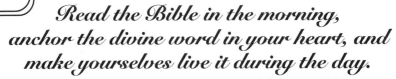

*Read the Bible in the morning,
anchor the divine word in your heart, and
make yourselves live it during the day.*

—Medjugorje, 1984

❦

They said to each other, "Were not our hearts burning within us while [Jesus]
was talking to us on the road, while he was opening the scriptures to us?"

—Luke 24:32

*Mary's insistence on the scriptures as a model for our lives is an intense one. She lived
her own life by the light of the Hebrew scriptures of the Jewish people, and her own
recollections came to be incorporated into the Christian scriptures. She understands,
better than any of us, who—and what—constitutes the word of God.*

When you pray,
do not keep looking at your watch.

—Medjugorje, 1983

Every generous act of giving, with every perfect gift, is from above, coming down from the Father of lights, with whom there is no variation or shadow due to change.

—James 1:17

Mary never knew what a watch was while she lived on earth, but from her vantage point she has undoubtedly seen many people looking at theirs, wondering how much longer the sermon or the prayer would take. She reminds us that in the kingdom of God, time is an irrelevant concept. Since we are made for eternity, perhaps we should look less often at our watches and more often at our spirits.

Prayer is life.

—Medjugorje, 1984

Choose life so that you and your descendants may live, loving the Lord your God, obeying him, and holding fast to him; for that means life to you and length of days, so that you may live in the land that the Lord swore to give to your ancestors, to Abraham, to Isaac, and to Jacob.

—Deuteronomy 30:19-20

Within our physical spacesuits, each designed to enable us to live on planet Earth, is an immortal spirit. Our spacesuits must be nourished with food and water of the earth, but our spirits cannot be nourished except through prayer. We can feed our bodies, only to have our spirits rise up in protest, crying out, "Feed me, too. I'm hungry!" Mary urges us to seek nourishment from God before our spirits starve.

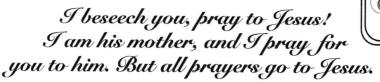

I beseech you, pray to Jesus!
I am his mother, and I pray for
you to him. But all prayers go to Jesus.

—Medjugorje (undated)

Therefore, since we are surrounded by so great a cloud of witnesses, let us also lay aside every weight and the sin that clings so closely, and let us run with perseverance the race that is set before us, looking to Jesus the pioneer and perfecter of our faith, who for the sake of the joy that was set before him endured the cross, disregarding its shame, and has taken his seat at the right hand of the throne of God.

—Hebrews 12:1-2

A priest asked if it were preferable to pray to her or directly to Jesus. Her reply was terse and emotional. Only God can be worshiped, and Mary is not divine. But if we ask our friends here on earth to pray for us, shouldn't we ask Mary, who loves all people and sees herself as their mother, to pray for us as well?

The best way to pray is . . . simply to do it.

—Medjugorje, 1984

❀

But whenever you pray, go into your room and shut the door and pray to your Father who is in secret; and your Father who sees in secret will reward you.

—*Matthew 6:6*

We can make the easiest things difficult! None of us has problems talking to our close family and friends. Yet when we think of praying to God, who should be our best friend of all, we make it a real problem. How do you talk to someone, whether God or anyone else? By beginning the conversation. That's all it takes. Mary knew that.

PEACE

Please stop fighting against each other. Join your forces and fight together for God.

—*Scottsdale, 1988*

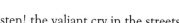

Listen! the valiant cry in the streets; the angels of peace weep bitterly. The highways are deserted, travelers have quit the road. The treaty is broken, its oaths are despised, its obligation is disregarded. The land mourns and languishes; Lebanon is confounded and withers away; Sharon is like a desert; and Bashan and Carmel shake off their leaves.

—*Isaiah 33:7-9*

Next to prayer, the Blessed Mother urges all people to pray and work for peace. Prayer alone is not enough. But as she has told us at Medjugorje and elsewhere, prayer can avert wars and catastrophes.

Please! Pray for peace!
This world will change with your prayers.

—Scottsdale, 1988

The effect of righteousness will be peace, and the result of righteousness, quietness and trust forever. My people will abide in a peaceful habitation, in secure dwellings, and in quiet resting places.

—Isaiah 32:17-18

How often have we heard that prayer changes things? And we say, Yes, maybe little things, an attitude adjustment here and there—but not big changes. Mary tells us otherwise: that prayer <u>can</u> bring peace, and peace <u>will</u> change the face of the world.

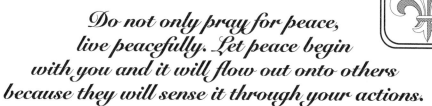

*Do not only pray for peace,
live peacefully. Let peace begin
with you and it will flow out onto others
because they will sense it through your actions.*

—*Scottsdale, 1988*

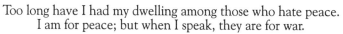

Too long have I had my dwelling among those who hate peace.
I am for peace; but when I speak, they are for war.

—*Psalms 120:6-7*

*The Blessed Mother reminds us that peace comes about not just through prayer but by
our own working and living in peace. When peace is firmly established in each heart,
then no one will want to take up arms against another.*

Love one another;
forgive each other; make peace. It is not
enough to ask for peace; make peace.

—Bernardo Martinez, Cuapa,
Nicaragua, 1980

But the wisdom from above is first pure, then peaceable, gentle, willing to yield, full of mercy and good fruits, without a trace of partiality or hypocrisy. And a harvest of righteousness is sown in peace for those who make peace.

—James 3:17-18

Jesus himself said, "Blessed are the peacemakers, for they will be called the children of God." Making peace involves love for others and forgiveness, both in receiving and in asking forgiveness. When we give up our resentments and anger at others, we can become reservoirs of peace for the thirsty of the world.

Do not turn to violence.
Never have recourse to violence.

—Bernardo Martinez, Cuapa,
Nicaragua, 1980

Thus says the Lord: Act with justice and righteousness, and deliver from the hand of the oppressor anyone who has been robbed. And do no wrong or violence . . .

—Jeremiah 22:3

Mary is above all a woman of peace. She has never claimed that she stood ready to hurl God's thunderbolts at humanity. She warns of wars and violence often, but they are the evils we inflict on others. When I was in college, my favorite saying was, "Suppose they gave a war and nobody came." Suppose we all decided to choose the path of peace. What a world we could live in then!

*My children, I, your most
holy mother, have come to ask
for peace. It is for that purpose that I speak
in many places over the entire world.*

—Elba and Zendia, Terra
Blanca, Mexico, 1987

Pray for the peace of Jerusalem: "May they prosper who love you. Peace be
within your walls, and security within your towers." For the sake of my
relatives and friends I will say, "Peace be within you." For the sake of the
house of the Lord our God, I will seek your good.

—Psalms 122:6-9

*Mary doesn't often talk about herself in such global language as this. She reminds us that
all her appearances are interconnected, woven together in the plan of God to bring the
world back to that plan—and to peace.*

*Take courage—the courage
to cultivate and to achieve peace.*

—Medjugorje, 1981

I believe that I shall see the goodness of the Lord in the land of the living.
Wait for the Lord; be strong, and let your heart take courage;
wait for the Lord!

—Psalms 27:13-14

*Mary reminds us that in a world climate that often approves or condones violence and
war, peace requires courage to pursue. At Medjugorje, Mary is speaking to some of the
most war-torn families and people of the world. If the people of Medjugorje can seek and
work for peace, then surely others can, too.*

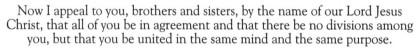

The Church is the Kingdom of God on earth. Whoever divided it has done wrong, and whoever rejoiced in its division has done wrong.

—*Soufanieh, 1983*

❀

Now I appeal to you, brothers and sisters, by the name of our Lord Jesus Christ, that all of you be in agreement and that there be no divisions among you, but that you be united in the same mind and the same purpose.

—*1 Corinthians 1:10*

Mary is a model of unity for all people. In Syria, where Orthodox and Catholic are often at odds over historical differences, she reminds all that while there can be differences in belief and practice, outright divisions are never part of God's plan.

LIFE

Please be on your best behavior.

—*Scottsdale, 1988*

But as for you, teach what is consistent with sound doctrine. Tell the older men to be temperate, serious, prudent, and sound in faith, in love, and in endurance. Likewise, tell the older women to be reverent in behavior, not to be slanderers or slaves to drink; they are to teach what is good.

—*Titus 2:1-3*

What a motherly statement to make! Mary reminds us that how we act is important; if we are to be witnesses to love, we must always behave in loving ways.

Revive the holiness of the family. Love each other.

—Julia Kim, Naju, Korea, 1985

❀

For this reason I bow my knees before the Father, from whom every family in heaven and on earth takes its name.

—*Ephesians 3:14-15*

The Holy Family of Nazareth—Mary, Joseph, and Jesus—has long been held up as a model of what every family should be like. For St. Paul, the fatherhood of God was the perfect model. In Mary's day, the Jewish woman had no legal power, yet she was the heart of the home. Two thousand years later, Mary is still calling families to be modeled on the divine family of God the Father, the mothering Spirit, and Jesus the obedient son.

People rely on their own knowledge, which they think is their source of greatness. They forget where that knowledge comes from.

—*Scottsdale, 1988*

He humbled you by letting you hunger, then by feeding you with manna, with which neither you nor your ancestors were acquainted, in order to make you understand that one does not live by bread alone, but by every word that comes from the mouth of the Lord.

—*Deuteronomy 8:3*

Mary's humility has always been evident from the first words of her hymn of praise. And as she reminds us in this message, humility is not making little of our talents and abilities, but in knowing that the source of all we have is God.

Experience the beauty of simplicity.

—*Scottsdale, 1988*

O Lord, my heart is not lifted up, my eyes are not raised too high; I do not occupy myself with things too great and too marvelous for me. But I have calmed and quieted my soul, like a weaned child with its mother; my soul is like the weaned child that is with me.

—*Psalms 131:1-2*

Mary herself might have written words like those of the old Shaker hymn: "'Tis a gift to be simple, 'tis a gift to be free, a gift to come down where we ought to be. And when we find ourselves in the place just right, it will be in the valley of love and delight. When true simplicity is gained, to bow and to bend we shall not be ashamed. To turn, turn will be our delight, till by turning, turning we come 'round right."

Mary's Little Instruction Book / 106

*I wish for you to continue
to remain open-hearted. Remember
that you have the choice every day to open
your hearts.*

—Scottsdale, 1989

Listen! I am standing at the door, knocking; if you hear my voice and open
the door, I will come in to you and eat with you, and you with me.

—Revelation 3:20

*When I first began to write books about angels, I would sign the books and add a winged
heart with a halo and a cross. But I never could draw the heart neatly closed at the
bottom. Then one day my angel said, "You realize, of course, that if you close your heart
up, you can't let love either in or out." —I've never tried to draw a closed heart since.*

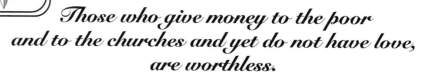

*Those who give money to the poor
and to the churches and yet do not have love,
are worthless.*

—*Soufanieh, 1982*

If I give away all my possessions, and if I hand over my body so that I may boast, but do not have love, I gain nothing.

—*1 Corinthians 13:3*

Mary reminds us that our intentions are all-important factors in our spiritual growth. Jesus said of people who gave alms with a great show and public spectacle, "They have already received their reward." We should remember that we need to give with love and caring, not because we want to be noticed and congratulated for our generosity.

Teach these words to all generations: unity, love, and faith.

—*Soufanieh, 1983*

I therefore, the prisoner in the Lord, beg you to lead a life worthy of the calling to which you have been called, with all humility and gentleness, with patience, bearing with one another in love, making every effort to maintain the unity of the Spirit in the bond of peace.

—*Ephesians 4:1-3*

St. Paul, writing from prison to the Ephesians, urges his readers, out of their faith, to live in unity and love. Mary, speaking to Myrna, urges the same. This is striking, given the serious religious differences, not only between different Christian churches in Syria, but between the Christian and Muslim communities. Mary's words cut across all religious and doctrinal levels to urge us to love in peace.

*Disconnect the television,
put aside all useless things.
I invite you to turn over your hearts.*

—Medjugorje, 1986

And Samuel said to the people, "Do not be afraid; you have done all this evil, yet do not turn aside from following the Lord, but serve the Lord with all your heart; and do not turn aside after useless things that cannot profit or save, for they are useless. For the Lord will not cast away his people, for his great name's sake, because it has pleased the Lord to make you a people for himself."

—1 Samuel 12:20-22

Mary's call at Medjugorje includes a strengthened prayer life, fasting on two days a week, and giving up many conveniences and entertainments in favor of building stronger families and greater faith. Perhaps we could try unplugging the TV set one day a week to start, and do things together instead.

I am with you, but I cannot deprive you of your freedom.

—Medjugorje, 1985

❊

For freedom Christ has set us free. Stand firm, therefore, and do not submit
again to a yoke of slavery.

—Galatians 5:1

*Mary herself learned that God intends for us to be gloriously free, to experience what St.
Paul calls in the letter to the Romans "the liberty of the children of God," when the angel
Gabriel was sent to her. Gabriel asked if she would consent to becoming the mother of
Jesus, but he did not compel or force her. Mary remained free to consent or to say no.
We, too, must choose to seek a way of life that seeks the face of God. We can, if we
choose, say no. But I think it is better if we always say yes to God as Mary did.*

Abide in joy. It is my desire.
Let joy appear on your faces.

—Medjugorje, 1981

❀

You show me the path of life. In your presence there is fullness of joy; in your right hand are pleasures forevermore.

—Psalms 16:11

Because Mary often speaks of sin and the necessity of doing penance, of making reparation, many people associate her messages with gloom and a hair-shirt style of life. But nothing could be further from the truth. Mary, in imitation of her son, wants for us a life filled with joy so strong that we cannot keep a smile off our face.

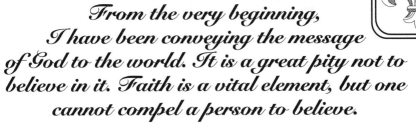

From the very beginning,
I have been conveying the message
of God to the world. It is a great pity not to
believe in it. Faith is a vital element, but one
cannot compel a person to believe.

—Medjugorje (undated)

❀

Now faith is the assurance of things hoped for,
the conviction of things not seen.

—Hebrews 11:1

Ivan, one of the visionaries, asked the Blessed Mother how to convince nonbelievers of
the reality of her visitations. She reminded him of the truth of the old saying,
"For those who believe, no explanations are necessary; for those who do not believe,
no explanations are possible."

We go to heaven in full consciousness, as we are now. At the moment of death, we are aware of the separation of the body and the soul.

—Medjugorje, 1982

✾

Indeed, the word of God is living and active, sharper than any two-edged sword, piercing until it divides soul from spirit, joints from marrow; it is able to judge the thoughts and intentions of the heart. And before him no creature is hidden, but all are naked and laid bare to the eyes of the one to whom we must render an account.

—Hebrews 4:12-13

I often hear stories from people who have been at the bedside of loved ones as they died. And they tell me that just before they died, as the eyes of their body clouded over, the eyes of their spirit saw through the veil and called upon the angels, other loved ones, and Jesus, whom they saw, and that they passed over with peace and joy.

It is false to teach people that we are reborn many times and that we pass to different bodies. One is born only once.

—Medjugorje, 1982

❧

And just as it is appointed for mortals to die once, and after that the judgment, so Christ, having been offered once to bear the sins of many, will appear a second time, not to deal with sin, but to save those who are eagerly waiting for him.

—Hebrews 9:27-28

Mary brings us many messages designed to warn against great spiritual evils, particularly the current fascination with reincarnation. Many believe that at her death, Mary was taken up to heaven body and soul together, one of few humans not to experience the separation of flesh and spirit.

You say, "It's raining too hard to go to church." Never speak like that! You always pray to God to send the rain that makes the earth rich. Then do not turn against the blessing from God.

—Medjugorje, 1984

For as the rain and the snow come down from heaven, and do not return there until they have watered the earth, making it bring forth and sprout, giving seed to the sower and bread to the eater, so shall my word be that goes out from my mouth.

—Isaiah 55:10-1

Mary reminds us that the weather itself is a creation of God designed for our great benefit, for the greening of the earth and the growth of its plants. Surely we should give thanks for the weather, whether or not it is to our liking.

Do not look with scorn
on the poor man who is begging
a morsel of bread from your abundant table.
Help him, and God will help you.

—Medjugorje, 1987

What good is it if you say you have faith but do not have works? If a brother or sister is naked and lacks daily food, and one of you says to them, "Go in peace; keep warm and eat your fill," and yet you do not supply their bodily needs, what is the good of that? So faith by itself, if it has no works, is dead.

—James 2:14-17

Mary cries out from the four corners of the world in these days, telling us to relieve the needs of the poor. Bosnia itself is desperately poor, apart from a few places that benefit from the many visitors and pilgrims to Medjugorje, yet Mary asks these very people to give to help the poor. Surely, if you had enough money to purchase this book, you have enough to help fill a need or a stomach somewhere. Make Mary happy.

I cannot cure.
God alone cures. I am not God!

—Medjugorje (undated)

❀

Jesus went throughout Galilee, teaching in their synagogues and proclaiming the good news of the kingdom and curing every disease and every sickness among the people. So his fame spread throughout all Syria, and they brought to him all the sick, those who were afflicted with various diseases and pains, demoniacs, epileptics, and paralytics, and he cured them.

—Matthew 4:2-34

This response came in answer to a question about whether she is responsible for the many healings that have happened in Medjugorje.

When you fall, you must not remain sitting; you must get up. The greatest fault is when you realize you have fallen and you don't get up.

—Ecuador, 1989

Now to him who is able to keep you from falling, and to make you stand without blemish in the presence of his glory with rejoicing, to the only God our Savior, through Jesus Christ our Lord, be glory, majesty, power, and authority, before all time and now and forever. Amen.

—Jude 1:24-5

How well Mary understands the need for courage! After all, she was there on Golgotha when her son died. She probably comforted Peter, who denied he even knew Jesus when his own life was threatened. We need to keep moving forward, even if we do stumble, knowing that the hand of God is ready to help us up again.

LOVE

You will experience happiness by loving one another.

—*Scottsdale, 1988*

❀

In this is love, not that we loved God but that he loved us and sent his Son to be the atoning sacrifice for our sins. Beloved, since God loved us so much, we also ought to love one another.

—*1 John 4:10-11*

Mary reminds us that love achieves its highest expression when it reaches out to others. It's right and necessary that we love ourselves and all God has given us. But it's even more necessary for us to be outgoing with our love, to pour it out on others, without reserve and without measure. The more love you give away, the happier you will be.

Love is a deep passion which flows with purity.

—*Scottsdale, 1988*

Set me as a seal upon your heart, as a seal upon your arm;
for love is strong as death, passion fierce as the grave.
Its flashes are flashes of fire, a raging flame.

—*Song of Songs 8:6*

We tend to make Mary a kind of two-dimensional holy card—pretty and devout, but without any particular depth, like the garish colors often used to paint her. But beneath the graceful robes and serene face, Mary is a woman of deep passion who can, and does, argue, cajole, plead, warn, and beg her children to follow God with all their hearts.

Allow your love to be shared by passing it on through your words, actions, and deeds.

—Scottsdale, 1988

Then Jesus poured water into a basin and began to wash the disciples' feet and to wipe them with the towel that was tied around him. He came to Simon Peter, who said to him, "Lord, are you going to wash my feet?" Jesus answered, "You do not know now what I am doing, but later you will understand." Peter said to him, "You will never wash my feet." Jesus answered, "Unless I wash you, you have no share with me."

—John 13:5-8

An old song from the '60s, which was much sung in churches, pointed out that since the Lord of love has come into our lives, we want to "pass it on"—the love, that is. Love, by its very nature, must be shared. Mary reminds us until we give love away, what we have is only a half-hearted love.

Return to basic principles of loving and respecting one another.

—*Scottsdale, 1988*

Those who say, "I love God," and hate their brothers or sisters, are liars; for those who do not love a brother or sister whom they have seen, cannot love God whom they have not seen.

—*1 John 4:20*

Mary's words in Scottsdale might have come from any mother or father or other elder whose eyes have seen a different age, when the "old-fashioned" values of simple respect for others and for life were more widely practiced than today. Mary's eyes have seen hundreds of generations, and she knows we need to return to the important values we have all but discarded. Let every day be a day to respect life in all its forms.

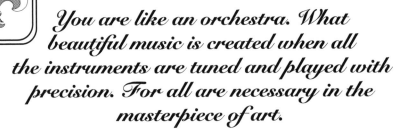

You are like an orchestra. What beautiful music is created when all the instruments are tuned and played with precision. For all are necessary in the masterpiece of art.

—Scottsdale, 1989

❀

For as in one body we have many members, and not all the members have the same function, so we, who are many, are one body in Christ, and individually we are members one of another.

—Romans 12:4-5

We are all part of the song that God sings to the world. Each of us has notes and melodies that no one else can play. Mary's role in the orchestra was like that of a perfect flute played by God, whose clear words sound like a silver bell above the noise of the all too large percussion section!

*Love your Muslim brothers
and sisters. Love your Serbian
Orthodox brothers and sisters. Love those
who govern you.*

—Medjugorje

Honor everyone. Love the family of believers.
Fear God. Honor the emperor.

—1 Peter 2:17

Medjugorje lies in the middle of an area of the world torn for centuries by religious and ethnic strife. The visionaries at Medjugorje are Catholics, as are most of the pilgrims; and to them Mary speaks of loving others whose religious differences have in the past sparked hatred and even murder. I'm sure she would want us to broaden her words to include all people of whatever faith, ethnic background, or political persuasion.

GOD

Let God dwell in the deepest, most central part of your life.

—Scottsdale, 1988

I pray that, according to the riches of his glory, he may grant that you may be strengthened in your inner being with power through his Spirit, and that Christ may dwell in your hearts through faith, as you are being rooted and grounded in love.

—Ephesians 3:16-17

For Mary, Jesus was—and is—her life. Only when God is on the throne of our hearts can the kingdom within be governed wisely and in love. Mary's messages from God are designed to help us take our selfish egos out of the depths of our hearts, and place God there instead.

*Jesus my Son is never outdone
in his love.*

—Scottsdale, 1989

"This is my commandment, that you love one another as I have loved you. No one has greater love than this, to lay down one's life for one's friends."
—John 15:12-13

How many memories did Mary have of her son Jesus's love: the miracles he worked, the feeding of the five thousand, the raising of Lazarus and the widow's son, the freeing of people from bondage. And the greatest gift of all, his giving himself up to death for his people. How many more examples of love since then have Mary's eyes seen—all the wonders of God's love over two thousand years.

It is not the person without bread who is poor, but the person without God.

—Gladys Quiroga de Mota, San Nicolas, Argentina, 1987

"I am the bread of life. Your ancestors ate the manna in the wilderness, and they died. This is the bread that comes down from heaven, so that one may eat of it and not die. I am the living bread that came down from heaven. Whoever eats of this bread will live forever; and the bread that I will give for the life of the world is my flesh."

—John 6:48-51

Mary, as the daughter of a priestly family, married to a skilled professional carpenter, probably never knew hunger and want, but she was not a rich woman in the material sense, either. Yet she was infinitely rich, because she knew only God can satisfy the most basic hunger in the human soul.

My dear children, the sweetest drink that can pass your lips is the Word of God.

—Gladys Quiroga de Mota, San Nicolas, Argentina, 1987

Your word is a lamp to my feet and a light to my path.
—Psalms 119:105

Jesus is called the Word of God by John the Evangelist. It was that Word whom Mary nourished for nine months within her own womb. Is it any wonder that she would appreciate the need to be nourished herself by the Word of God?

When God comes among you he does not come for amusement. He is not afraid of either the powerful or the indifferent.

—Mafalda Mattia, Oliveto
Citra, Italy, 1986

Let the heavens praise your wonders, O Lord, your faithfulness in the assembly of the holy ones. For who in the skies can be compared to the Lord? Who among the heavenly beings is like the Lord, a God feared in the council of the holy ones, great and awesome above all that are around him? O Lord God of hosts, who is as mighty as you, O Lord? Your faithful ones surround you.

—Psalms 89:5-8

Mary's words remind us of the power and majesty of God, and of the divine purpose as well. For God is no dilettante to try this and dabble in that; God's purposes and plans are serious, and we need to pay attention when God speaks, either directly or through an angel or through the Blessed Mother or one of the saints.

MOTHER

I know you are tired, my children, but I, your mother, am tireless and wish to comfort you.

—Scottsdale, 1989

Comfort, O comfort my people, says your God.

—Isaiah 40:1

People all over the world, for twenty centuries have experienced the warmth of Mary's motherhood, from Jesus himself, to his disciple John, to millions in our own day. For a long time, I never felt I needed to turn to Mary as a mother figure. But after my own mother died, I began to look to Mary as a motherly human face always willing to listen and to add her own prayers to mine before God.

Do not see me, your mother,
as more blessed than you. All
who live in my Jesus are as blessed as I.

—*Scottsdale, 1989*

❁

Jesus said to them, "My mother and my brothers are those
who hear the word of God and do it."

—*Luke 8:21*

Mary's disarming humility was never more charming than in these words given in
Scottsdale. Mary is telling us that all of us have the right to sing the Magnificat with all
our hearts. Our destiny is the same as that of the Virgin Mary: to know and live in the
presence of God forever.

*On the day of the Annunciation,
I experienced unparalleled joy. I did not
understand, and yet my joy allowed me to
give my consent.*

—Gladys Quiroga de Mota, San
Nicolas, Argentina, 1987

When a woman is in labor, she has pain, because her hour has come. But when her child is born, she no longer remembers the anguish because of the joy of having brought a human being into the world.

—John 16:21

God is not a God of anger and violence, but a God of love and joy. And Mary reminds us that when God asks something of us, we are filled with joy so our Yes! can be as full and loving as was Mary's.

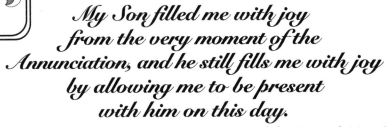

My Son filled me with joy
from the very moment of the
Annunciation, and he still fills me with joy
by allowing me to be present
with him on this day.

—Gladys Quiroga de Mota, San
Nicolas, Argentina, 1987

If you keep my commandments, you will abide in my love, just as I have kept
my Father's commandments and abide in his love. I have said these things to
you so that my joy may be in you, and that your joy may be complete.

—John 15:10-11

For me, the important part of his message is Mary's use of the word "allow." Mary, as an
obedient daughter of God, never claims more than her due. She is with us because God
permits; she is not an independent creature who does her own will; she never was. Her
only concern is to continue to hear the word of God and fulfill it.

Tell pilgrims I do not need candles and flowers. Let them pray . . .

—Tarcisio di Biasi, Oliveto
Citra, Italy, 1985

The angel of the Lord said to Manoah, "If you detain me,
I will not eat your food; but if you want to prepare a burnt offering,
then offer it to the Lord."

—Judges 13:16

People have offered Mary many things over the centuries. But Mary has no interest in receiving anything that might detract from the glory of God. She knows, better than some of us, she is purely and wonderfully human, and only human. She asks, instead of offerings, that people pray to her son, who alone grants our requests.

I hold you in my arms. . . .
I love you, I hold you
on my knees.

—Medjugorje, 1984

For thus says the Lord: I will extend prosperity to her like a river, and the wealth of the nations like an overflowing stream; and you shall nurse and be carried on her arm, and dandled on her knees. As a mother comforts her child, so I will comfort you; you shall be comforted in Jerusalem.

—Isaiah 66:12-13

Mary's tenderness is evident in this loving and supportive message from Medjugorje. Like any mother with her child, she expresses her love in deeply emotional terms, as a woman who feels intensely the needs of her children.

I am beautiful because I love.

—Medjugorje, 1984

You are altogether beautiful, my love; there is no flaw in you.
—Song of Songs 4:7

This simple and loving message was Mary's answer to Jelena, one of the little children who saw her and who asked, "Why are you so beautiful?"

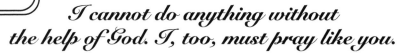

*I cannot do anything without
the help of God. I, too, must pray like you.*

—Medjugorje, 1982

❀

I write these things to you who believe in the name of the Son of God, so that
you may know that you have eternal life. And this is the boldness we have in
him, that if we ask anything according to his will, he hears us. And if we know
that he hears us in whatever we ask, we know that we have obtained the
requests made of him.

—1 John 5:13-15

*At certain times and in various places devotion to Mary sometimes went beyond the
bounds of the appropriate. Mary lets us know quite forcefully that she is a creature like
us, dependent on the providence of God. If only we could realize as strongly that all we
do depends on God's help, we could change the world.*

Mary's Little Instruction Book / 138

Notes

Medjugorje

Medjugorje is a town in Bosnia, part of the former Yugoslavia, where, for a number of years, the Virgin Mary has been appearing to a number of young people. Medjugorje has become a great pilgrimage site in spite of the war-torn region, and thousands of people have testified to having their faith renewed or restored after visiting the area. The messages in this book are taken from *Messages and Teachings of Mary at Medjugorje,* by René Laurentin and René LeJeune, The Riehle Foundation, P.O. Box 7, Milford, OH 45150, used with permission.

Soufanieh

Soufanieh is in Damascus, in the Syrian Arab Republic, where, since 1982, the Blessed Mother and Jesus have been speaking to Myrna al-Akhras, a local Syrian Catholic woman married to Nicholas Nazzour, a Greek Orthodox believer. Apart from the words Myrna hears, fragrant oil frequently appears on her hands or on an icon that is venerated by the faithful. So far there is no natural explanation for the appearance of the oil, to which have been attributed miraculous cures. The accounts are found in *Memoir: Our Lady of Soufanieh,* by Antoine Mansour and Claire Mansour, privately printed.

Scottsdale

St. Maria Goretti is a vibrant Catholic parish in Scottsdale, Arizona, with a large prayer group that meets regularly. Beginning in 1987, various members of the group began receiving messages from Mary and Jesus, which urge their hearers to give their lives to God more completely. The accounts are found in *I Am Your Jesus of Mercy,* Vol. 1, published by The Riehle Foundation, P.O. Box 7, Milford, OH 45150, and used with permission.

Oliveto Citra

A small town in Italy, Oliveto Citra has been the site of Marian apparitions to a group of townspeople since 1985. Various unusual phenomena, such as cloud formations and the appearance of stars, have accompanied the visions. Some of these messages have been collected in *Apparitions of the Blessed Virgin Mary Today,* by René Laurentin, Veritas, Dublin, 1991.

San Nicolas, Argentina

Near Buenos Aires, San Nicolas is the home of Gladys Quiroga de Mota, a mother who has been giving messages from the Blessed Mother since 1983. Some of these messages have been collected in *Apparitions of the Blessed Virgin Mary Today,* by René Laurentin, Veritas, Dublin, 1991.

Terra Blanca, Mexico

The two children who have seen the Virgin and who give her messages are poor peasant children, who, until recently, had barely enough education to write down the messages they have been given. Now attending a state school, the children have grown profoundly in their faith, according to their father. Some of these messages have been collected in *Apparitions of the Blessed Virgin Mary Today,* by René Laurentin, Veritas, Dublin, 1991.

Fatima, Portugal

In 1917 the Virgin Mary appeared several times to three peasant children named Lucia, Jacinta and Francisco, revealing to them certain secrets and asking for prayer and sacrifice to convert Russia to the Christian faith. Many bystanders witnessed the miracle of the "spinning sun" during the final visitation.

Ecuador

From 1989 a number of persons in Ecuador have been reporting words and visions of the Blessed Mother and Jesus. The messages are reported in *I Am the Guardian of the Faith*, by Sr. Isabel Bettwy, Franciscan U. Press, Steubenville, OH 43952.

Naju, Korea

Beginning in 1985, a statue of the Blessed Mother in the home of Julia and Julio Kim, two Korean converts to Catholicism, began to weep, and Julia was given messages from the Blessed Mother.

Cuapa, Nicaragua

In 1980 the Virgin Mary is said to have appeared to Bernardo Martinez, an adult laborer, giving him a message of peace that emphasized the need for people to take active steps toward securing world peace.

EILEEN ELIAS FREEMAN directs the activities of The Angel-Watch™ Foundation, Inc., and publishes the *AngelWatch*™ *Journal*. She is the author of the bestselling books *Touched by Angels*, *The Angels' Little Instruction Book*, and *Angelic Healing*. Eileen holds a master's degree in theology from the University of Notre Dame and a B.A. in comparative religion from Barnard College. For information about Angel-Watch, please send a stamped (or enclose two I.R.Cs for overseas mail), self-addressed envelope to The AngelWatch Foundation, P.O. Box 1397, Mountainside, NJ 07092.